Face Painting

Jacqueline Russon

CONTENTS

First things first

Next time you have a party, give a show, or just feel like dressing up, why not paint your face? Once you've tried the ten faces in the book, try making up your own.

All you need is ...

tissues for any mess

small brush for details

medium brush for outlines

big brush for filling in large areas

water-based paints in a box or separate pots

bowl of water

makeup sponge or bath sponge cut into pieces

Using a sponge
Wet the sponge. Squeeze out most of the water. Wipe it around the paint pot and then gently dab your face. Sponge your eyes last. Make sure they are closed.

Using a brush
Wet the brush and dip it into the paint. Be careful. If it is too wet, the paint will run. If it is too dry, it will pull on your skin.

Blending
Blending is a way of mixing two colors together. Sponge on one color first. Let it dry. Gently rub on the second color with a dry sponge or your fingers.

Cuddly teddy

Why not have a teddy bear picnic?

1 Sponge your face yellow all over. Blend reddish brown around the outside. Dab a little red on your cheeks.

2 Paint the tip of your nose black. Add a curly black mouth and little black whisker spots.

4

The colors you need are...

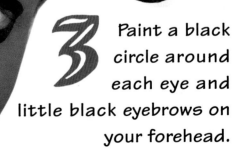

yellow

red

brown

black

3 Paint a black circle around each eye and little black eyebrows on your forehead.

Cheery clown

Turn somersaults and play some tricks!

1
Paint a huge, red smiley mouth. Sponge a red spot on your nose.

The colors you need are...

red blue yellow orange black green

2
Carefully paint bright-colored stripes over your eyelids. Add pointed black eyebrows over the stripes.

3 Sponge bright green spots on your cheeks. Paint multicolored dots above them.

Scary ghost

Here's a spooky face for Halloween.

1 Paint a white ghost shape over your face, like this.

2 Add a large black patch over each eye and another one over your nose.

The colors you need are...

white   black   green

3 Carefully color the rest of your face black. Paint wobbly green eyebrows above the eye patches.

Mini monster

Be careful not to scare the neighbors!

1 Paint a large yellow patch over each eye. Paint a pattern of bright green scales on your forehead, nose, cheeks, and chin.

2 Fill in the rest of your face with purple. Paint your lips dark red.

The colors you need are...

green

white

yellow

brown

red

purple

black

3

Paint white fangs on either side of your mouth and two little black nostrils on your nose. Add pointed eyebrows.

11

Funny bunny

Practice twitching your nose like a real rabbit.

1 Paint a pale pink arch over each eye. Sponge dark pink on the rest of your face.

2 Paint a gray feathery muzzle. Draw white teeth over your top and bottom lip. Leave to dry.

The colors you need are...

white   pale pink   dark pink   gray   black

3 Paint black eyebrows above the arches and add a black nose and whiskers.

Outline the teeth in black.

Shiny robot

Walk with stiff arms and legs just like a robot.

The colors you need are...

silver   dark gray   red   black

1 Color your whole face silver. Paint dark gray panels on your cheeks and forehead and triangles over your eyebrows.

2 Paint your lips and your eyelids bright red.

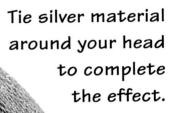

Tie silver material around your head to complete the effect.

Outline lips and shapes in black. Paint black screws with white flecks on the panels.

Stripy Cat

Prowl around the garden with this furry face.

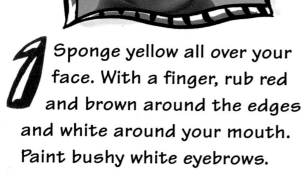

1 Sponge yellow all over your face. With a finger, rub red and brown around the edges and white around your mouth. Paint bushy white eyebrows.

2 Paint red, brown, and black stripes all around the outside of your face. Make long stripes on your forehead.

The colors you need are...

yellow
red
brown
white
black

16

3 Backcomb your hair to make it look wild and furry.

Paint lines on your nose and around your eyes and mouth. Add whiskers and a red mouth.

Watery mermaid

Decorate your hair with shells and sing sweetly!

1 Paint a green wavy base over part of your face, leaving a bare circle around each eye. Fill in the rest with white foamy waves.

2 Carefully paint pink, silver, and purple striped shells over your eyelids and eyebrows. Blend the colors together.

3 Sponge pink spots on your cheeks. Paint your lips purple.

The colors you need are...

green

white

pink

purple

silver

Spotty dog

Would you give this doggy a bone?

1 Sponge your face white. Paint black patches over both eyes. Dab spots on your chin, cheeks, and forehead.

2 Carefully paint a black nose tip and mouth. Add several black whisker spots.

The colors you need are...

black white red

3 Paint a bright red tongue hanging out of your mouth and black eyebrows.

If you have long hair, tie it in ponytails to make it look like long doggy ears.

21

Pretty Polly

You'll really stand out with this face!

1 Paint a yellow beak over your nose. Add dark green feather shapes on your forehead, eyebrows, and cheeks.

2 Add some red feathers. Paint red over your eyelids and put a red nostril on either side of your nose.

The colors you need are...

green

purple

red   yellow   orange

3

Paint purple and orange
feathers in between the
red and green ones.

Index

Copyright © 1996 by HarperCollins Publishers Ltd
This edition first published in 1997 by Carolrhoda Books, Inc.
First published in England in 1996 by HarperCollins Publishers Ltd, London.
All rights to this edition reserved by Carolrhoda Books, Inc. No part of this book may be reproduced, stored in a retrieval system, or transmitted in any form or by any means, electronic, mechanical, photocopying, recording, or otherwise, without the prior written permission of Carolrhoda Books, Inc., except for the inclusion of brief quotations in an acknowledged review.
Carolrhoda Books, Inc., c/o The Lerner Publishing Group
241 First Avenue North, Minneapolis, MN 55401 U.S.A.
Library of Congress Cataloging-in-Publication Data
Russon, Jacqueline.
Face painting / Jacqueline Russon ;
[illustrations by Mei Lim ; photographs by Steve Shott].
    p.   cm.
Includes index.
Summary: Provides instructions for creating ten different faces, including a cuddly teddy, funny bunny, stripy cat, and watery mermaid.
ISBN 1-57505-099-4
1. Face painting—Juvenile literature. [1. Face painting.]
I. Lim, Mei, ill. II. Shott, Stephen, ill. III. Title.
TT911.R87 1997
745.5—dc21   96-37361
Printed in Hong Kong
Bound in the United States of America
1 2 3 4 5 6 OS 02 01 00 99 98 97

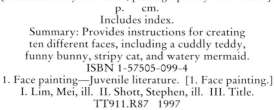